Agesilaus

An Encomium

Xenophon

Translated by Henry Dakyns

**Published in London
1892**

TABLE OF CONTENTS

The date of Agesilaus's death is uncertain — 360 B.C. (Grote, "H. G." ix. 336); 358 B.C. (Curt. iv. 196, Eng. tr.)

I

To write the praises of Agesilaus in language equalling his virtue and renown is, I know, no easy task; yet must it be essayed; since it were but an ill requital of pre-eminence, that, on the ground of his perfection, a good man should forfeit the tribute even of imperfect praise.

As touching, therefore, the excellency of his birth, what weightier, what nobler testimony can be adduced than this one fact? To the commemorative list of famous ancestry is added today the name[1]Agesilaus as holding this or that numerical descent from Heracles, and these ancestors no private persons, but kings sprung from the loins of kings. Nor is it open to the gainsayer to contend that they were kings indeed but of some chance city. Not so, but even as their family holds highest honour in their fatherland, so too is their city the most glorious in Hellas, whereby they hold, not primacy over the second best, but among leaders they have leadership.

And herein it is open to us to praise both his fatherland and his family. It is notable that never throughout these ages has Lacedaemon, out of envy of the privilege accorded to her kings, tried to dissolve their rule; nor ever yet throughout these ages have her kings strained after greater powers than those which limited their heritage of kingship from the first. Wherefore, while all other forms of government, democracies and oligarchies, tyrannies and monarchies, alike have failed to maintain their continuity unbroken, here, as the sole exception, endures indissolubly their kingship.[2]

And next in token of an aptitude for kingship seen in Agesilaus, before even he entered upon office, I note these signs. On the death of Agis, king of Lacedaemon, there were rival claimants to the throne. Leotychides claimed the succession as being the son of Agis, and Agesilaus as the son of Archidamus. But the verdict of Lacedaemon favoured Agesilaus as being in point of family and virtue unimpeachable,[3] and so they set him on the throne. And yet, in this princeliest of cities so to be selected by the noblest citizens as worthy of highest privilege, argues, methinks conclusively, an excellence forerunning exercise of rule.[4]

And so I pass on at once to narrate the chief achievements of his reign, since by the light of deeds the character of him who wrought them will, if I mistake not, best shine forth.

Agesilaus was still a youth[5] when he obtained the kingdom, and he was still but a novice in his office when the news came that the king of Persia was collecting a mighty armament by sea and land for the invasion of Hellas. The Lacedaemonians and their allies sat debating these matters, when Agesilaus undertook to cross over into Asia. He only asked for thirty Spartans and two thousand New Citizens,[6] besides a contingent of the allies six thousand strong; with these he would cross over into Asia and endeavour to effect a peace; or, if the barbarian preferred war, he would leave him little leisure to invade Hellas.

The proposal was welcomed with enthusiasm on the part of many. They could not but admire the eagerness of their king to retaliate upon the Persian for his former invasions of Hellas by counter-invasion on his own soil. They liked the preference also which he showed for attacking rather than awaiting his enemy's attack, and his intention to carry on the war at the expense of Persia rather than that of Hellas; but it was the perfection of policy, they felt, so to change the arena of battle, with Asia as the prize of victory instead of Hellas. If we pass on to the moment when he had received his army and set sail, I can conceive no clearer exposition of his generalship than the bare narration of his exploits.

The scene is Asia, and this his first achievement. Tissaphernes had sworn an oath to Agesilaus on this wise: if Agesilaus would grant him an armistice until the return of certain ambassadors whom he would send to the king, he (Tissaphernes) would do his utmost to procure the independence of the Hellenic cities in Asia. And Agesilaus took a counter oath: without fraud or covin to observe the armistice during the three months^z necessary to that transaction. But the compact was scarcely made when Tissaphernes gave the lie to the solemn undertaking he had sworn to. So far from effecting peace, he begged the King to send him a large armament in addition to that which he already had. As to Agesilaus, though he was well aware of these proceedings, he adhered loyally to the armistice.

And for myself, I look upon this as the first glorious achievement of the Spartan. By displaying the perjury of Tissaphernes he robbed him of his credit with all the world; by the exhibition of himself in contrast as a man who ratified his oath and would not gainsay an article of his agreement, he gave all men, Hellenes and barbarians alike, encouragement to make covenant with him to the full extent of his desire.

When Tissaphernes, priding himself on the strength of that army which had come down to aid him, bade Agesilaus to be gone from Asia or to prepare for war,[8] deep was the vexation depicted on the faces of the Lacedaemonians there present and their allies, as they realised that the scanty force of Agesilaus was all too small to cope with the armaments of Persia. But the brow of their general was lit with joy as gaily he bade the ambassadors take back this answer to Tissaphernes: "I hold myself indebted to your master for the perjury whereby he has obtained to himself the hostility of heaven, and made the gods themselves allies of Hellas." And so without further pause he published a general order to his soldiers to pack their baggage and prepare for active service; and to the several cities which lay on the line of march to Caria, the order sped to have their markets in readiness; while to the men of Ionia and the Aeolid and the Hellespont he sent despatches bidding them send their contingents to Ephesus to join in the campaign.

Tissaphernes meanwhile was influenced by the fact that Agesilaus had no cavalry, and that Caria was a hilly district unsuited for that arm. Moreover, as he further bethought him, Agesilaus must needs be wroth with him for his deceit. What could be clearer, therefore, than that he was about to make a dash at the satrap's home in Caria? Accordingly he transported the whole of his infantry into Caria and marched his cavalry round the while into the plain of the Maeander, persuaded that he would trample the Hellenes under the hoofs of his horses long before they reached the district where no cavalry could operate.

But Agesilaus, instead of advancing upon Caria, turned right about and marched in the direction of Phrygia. Picking up the various forces that met him on his progress, he passed onwards, laying city after city at his feet, and by the suddenness of his incursion capturing enormous wealth.

Here was an achievement which showed the genius of a general, as all agreed. When once war as declared, and the arts of circumvention and deceit were thereby justified, he had proved Tissaphernes to be a very bade in subtlety;[9] and with what sagacity again did he turn the circumstances to account for the enrichment of his friends. Owing to the quantity of wealth captured, precious things were selling for a mere song. Thereupon he gave his friends warning to make their purchases, adding that he should at once march down to the sea-coast at the head of his troops. The quartermasters meanwhile received orders to make a note of the purchasers with the prices of the articles, and to consign the goods. The result was that, without prior disbursement on their part, or detriment to the public treasury, his friends reaped an enormous harvest. Moreover, when deserters came with offers to disclose hidden treasures, and naturally enough laid their proposal before the king himself, he took care to have the capture of these treasures effected by his friends, which would enable them to do a stroke of business, and at the same time redound to their prestige. For this reason he was not long in discovering many an eager aspirant to his friendship.

But a country pillaged and denuded of inhabitants would not long support an army. That he felt. A more perennial source of supply was surely to be found in waving cornfields and thickly clustering homesteads. So with infinite pains he set himself not merely to crush his foes by force, but also to win them to his side by gentleness. In this spirit he often enjoined upon his soldiers to guard their captives as fellow-men rather than take vengeance upon them as evildoers;[10] or, on a change of quarters, if aware of little children left behind by the dealers (since the men often sold them in the belief that it would be impossible to carry them away and rear them), he would show concern in behalf of these poor waifs and have them conveyed to some place of safety; or he would entrust them to the care of fellow-prisoners also left behind on account of old age; in no case must they be left to ravening dogs and wolves. In this way he won the goodwill not only of those who heard tell of these doings but of the prisoners themselves. And whenever he brought over a city to his side, he set the citizens free from the harsher service of a bondsman to his lord, imposing the gentler obedience of a freeman to his ruler. Indeed, there were fortresses impregnable to assault which he brought under his power by the subtler force of human kindness.

But when, in Phrygia even, the freedom of his march along the flats was hampered by the cavalry of Pharnabazus, he saw that if he wished to avoid a skulking warfare under cover, a force of cavalry was indispensable. Accordingly he enlisted the wealthiest members of every city in those parts to breed and furnish horses; with this saving clause, however: that the individual who furnished a horse and arms with a good rider should be exempt from service himself. By this means he engendered an eagerness to discharge the obligation, not unlike that of the condemned man, casting about to discover some one to die in his place.[11] He further ordered some of the states themselves to furnish contingents of mounted troopers, and this in the conviction that from such training-centres he would presently get a pick of cavaliers proud of their horsemanship. And thus once more he won golden opinions by the skill with which he provided himself with a body of cavalry in the plenitude of strength and ripe for active service.

On the approach of early spring[12] he collected his whole armament at Ephesus, and set himself to the work of training it. With that object he proposed a series of prizes: one set for the cavalry squadron which rode best, another for the heavy infantry divisions which presented the best physique, another again for various light troops, peltasts, and bowmen, which showed themselves most efficient in their respective duties.

Thereupon it was a sight to see the gymnasiums thronged with warriors going through their exercises, the racecourses crowded with troopers on prancing steeds, the archers and the javelin men shooting at the butts. Nay, the whole city in which he lay was transformed into a spectacle itself, so filled to overflowing was the market-place with arms and armour of every sort, and horses, all for sale. Here were coppersmiths and carpenters, ironfounders and cobblers, painters and decorators — one and all busily engaged in fabricating the implements of war; so that an onlooker might have thought the city of Ephesus itself a gigantic arsenal. It would have kindled courage in the breast of a coward to see the long lines of soldiers, with Agesilaus at their head, all garlanded as they marched in proud procession from the gymnasiums and dedicated their wreaths to our Lady Artemis. Since, where these three elements exist — reverence towards heaven, practice in military affairs, and obedience to command — all else must needs be full of happy promise.

But seeing that contempt for the foe is calculated to infuse a certain strength in face of battle, he ordered his criers to strip naked the barbarians captured by his foraging parties, and so to sell them. The soldiers who saw the white skins of these folk, unused to strip for toil, soft and sleek and lazy-looking, as of people who could only stir abroad in carriages, concluded that a war with women would scarcely be more formidable. Then he published a further order to the soldiers: "I shall lead you at once by the shortest route to the stronghold[13] of the enemy's territory. Your general asks you to keep yourselves on the alert in mind and body, as men about to enter the lists of battle on the instant."

But Tissaphernes was persuaded that this was all talk on his part for the purpose of outwitting him a second time: now certainly Agesilaus would make an incursion into Caria. So once again the satrap transported his infantry over into that country just has he had done before, and as before he posted his cavalry in the plain of the Maeander.

This time, however, Agesilaus was true to his word. In accordance with his published order he advanced straight upon the region of Sardis, and, during a three days' march through a country where not an enemy was to be seen, provided his army with abundant supplies. On the fourth day the enemy's cavalry came up. The Persian general ordered the commandant of his baggage train to cross the Pactolus and encamp, whilst his troopers, who had caught sight of the camp followers of the Hellenes scattered in search of booty, put many of them to the sword. Agesilaus, aware how matters were going, ordered his cavalry to the rescue, and the Persians on their side, seeing the enemy's supports approaching, collected and formed up in line to receive them with the serried squadrons of their cavalry. And now Agesilaus, conscious that his enemy's infantry had not as yet arrived, whilst on his side no element in his preparation was lacking, felt that the moment was come to join battle if he could. Accordingly he sacrificed and advanced against the opposing lines of cavalry. A detachment of heavy infantry, the ten-years-service men, had orders to close with them at the run, while the light infantry division were told to show them the way at a swinging pace. At the same time he passed the order along the line of his cavalry to charge in reliance of the support of himself and the main body in their rear. Charge they did, these troopers, and the pick of Persian cavalry received them bravely, but in face of the conjoint horror of the attack they swerved, and some were cut down at once in the river-bed, while others sought safety in flight. The Hellenes followed close on the heels of the flying foe, and captured his camp. Here the peltasts, not unnaturally, fell to pillaging, whereupon Agesilaus formed a cordon of troops, round the property of friends and foes alike, and so encamped.

Presently hearing that the enemy were in a state of disorder, the result of every one holding his fellow responsible for what had happened, he advanced without further stay on Sardis. Having arrived, he fell to burning and ravaging the suburbs, while at the same time he did not fail to make it known by proclamation that those who asked for freedom should join his standard; or if there were any who claimed a right of property in Asia he challenged them to come out and meet her liberators in fair fight and let the sword decide between them. Finding that no one ventured to come out to meet him, his march became for the future a peaceful progress. All around him he beheld Hellenes who formerly were forced to bow the knee to brutal governors now honoured by their former tyrants, while those who had claimed to enjoy divine honours were so humbled by him that they scarce dared to look a Hellene in the face. Everywhere he saved the territory of his friends from devastation, and reaped the fruits of the enemy's soil to such good effect that within two years he was able to dedicate as a tithe to the god at Delphi more than one hundred talents.[14]

It was then that the Persian king, believing that Tissaphernes was to blame for the ill success of his affairs, sent down Tithraustes and cut off the satrap's head. After this the fortunes of the barbarians grew still more desperate, whilst those of Agesilaus assumed a bolder front. On all side embassies from the surrounding nations came to make terms of friendship, and numbers even came over to him, stretching out eager arms to grasp at freedom. So that Agesilaus was now no longer the chosen captain of the Hellenes only, but of many Asiatics.

And here we may pause and consider what a weight of admiration is due to one who, being now ruler over countless cities of the continent, and islands also (since the state had further entrusted the navy to his hands), just when he had reached this pinnacle of renown and power, and might look to turn to account his thronging fortunes; when, too, which overtops all else, he was cherishing fond hopes to dissolve that empire which in former days had dared to march on Hellas; — at such a moment suffered himself not to be overmastered by these promptings, but on receipt of a summons of the home authorities to come to the assistance of the fatherland, obeyed the mandate of his state as readily[15] as though he stood confronted face to face with the Five in the hall of ephors; and thus gave clear proof that he would not accept the whole earth in exchange for the land of his fathers, nor newly-acquired in place of ancient friends, nor base gains ingloriously purchased rather than the perilous pursuit of honour and uprightness.[16]

And, indeed, glancing back at the whole period during which he remained in the exercise of his authority, no act of deeper significance in proof of his kingly qualities need be named than this. He found the cities which he was sent out to govern each and all a prey to factions, the result of constitutional disturbances consequent on the cessation of the Athenian empire, and without resort to exile or sanguinary measures he so disposed them by his healing presence that civil concord and material prosperity were permanently maintained. Therefore it was that the Hellenes in Asia deplored his departure,[17] as though they had lost, not simply a ruler, but a father or bosom friend, and in the end they showed that their friendship was of no fictitious character. At any rate, they voluntarily helped him to succour Lacedaemon, though it involved, as they knew, the need of doing battle with combatants of equal prowess with themselves. So the tale of his achievements in Asia has an end.

[1] Or, "even today, in the proud bead-roll of his ancestry he stands commemorated, in numerical descent from Heracles."

[2] See "Cyrop." I. i. 1.

[3] For this matter see "Hell." III. iii. 1-6; V. iv. 13; Plut. "Ages." iii. 3 (Cloigh, iv. 3 foll.); Paus. iii. 3.

[4] See Aristides ("Rhet." 776), who quotes the passage for its measured cadence.

[5] B.C. 399; according to Plut. ("Ages." ad fin.) he was forty-three, and therefore still "not old." See "Hell." III. iv. 1 for the startling news, B.C. 396.

[6] For the class of Neodamodes, see Arnold's note to Thuc. v. 34 (Jowett, "Thuc." ii. 307); also Thuc. vii. 58; "Hell." I. iii. 15.

[7] See Grote, "H. G." x. 359; "Hell." III. iv. 5.

[8] Lit. "When Tissaphernes, priding himself . . . bade Agesilaus be gone . . . deep was the annoyance felt."

9 See below, xi. 4; "Mem." III. i. 6; IV. ii. 15; "Cyrop." I. vi. 31; Plut. "Ages." xi. (Clough, iv. 10).

10 See Grote, vol. ix. p. 365 foll.

11 Instead of the plain zetoie of the parallel passage ("Hell." III. iv. 15) the encomiast prefers the poetical masteuoi.

12 B.C. 395; see "Hell." III. iv. 16; Plut. "Marcel." (Clough, ii. 262); Polyb. xii. 20, 7.

13 Or, "the richest parts of the country," viz. Lydia; Plut. "Ages." x.

14 = 25,000 pounds nearly.

15 Cf. Hor. "Od." III. v. 50.

16 See Pindar, "Olymp." vi. 14.

17 See Plut. "Ages." xv.

II

He crossed the Hellespont and made his way through the very tribes traversed by the Persian[18] with his multitudinous equipment in former days, and the march which cost the barbarian a year was accomplished by Agesilaus in less than a single month. He did not want to arrive a day too late to serve his fatherland. And so passing through Macedonia he arrived in Thessaly, and here the men of Larissa, Crannon, Scotussa, and Pharsalus, who were allies of the Boeotians, and indeed all the Thessalians, with the exception of those who were in exile at the time, combined to dog his steps and do him damage. For a while he led his troops in a hollow square, posting one half of his cavalry in the van and the other half on his rear, but finding his march hindered by frequent attacks of the Thessalians on his hindmost divisions, he sent round the mass of his cavalry from the vanguard to support his rear, reserving' only his personal escort.[19] And now in battle order the rival squadrons faced each other; when the Thessalians, not liking a cavalry engagement in face of heavy infantry, wheeled and step by step retreated; their opponents with much demureness following. Then Agesilaus, detecting the common error under which both parties laboured, sent round his own bodyguard of stalwart troopers with orders to their predecessors (an order they would act upon themselves) to charge the enemy at full gallop and not give him a chance to rally. The Thessalians, in face of this unexpected charge, either could not so much as rally, or in the attempt to do so were caught with their horses' flanks exposed to the enemy's attack. Polycharmus, the Pharsalian, a commandant of cavalry, did indeed succeed in wheeling, but was cut down with those about him sword in hand. This was the signal for a flight so extraordinary that dead and dying lined the road, and the living were captured wholesale, nor was a halt made until the pursuers reached Mount Narthacius. Here, midway between Pras and Narthacius, Agesilaus erected a trophy, and here for the moment he halted in unfeigned satisfaction at his exploit, since it was from an antagonist boasting the finest cavalry in the world that he had wrested victory with a body of cavalry organised by himself.

Next day, crossing the mountain barrier of Achaea Phthiotis, his march lay through friendly territory for the rest of the way as far as the frontiers of Boeotia. Here he found the confederates drawn up in battle line. They consisted of the Thebans, the Athenians, the Argives, the Corinthians, the Aenianians, the Euboeans, and both divisions of the

Locrians.[20] He did not hesitate, but openly before their eyes drew out his lines to give them battle. He had with him a division[21] and a half of Lacedaemonians, and from the seat of war itself the allied troops of the Phocians and the men of Orchomenus only, besides the armament which he had brought with him from Asia.

I am not going to maintain that he ventured on the engagement in spite of having far fewer and inferior forces. Such an assertion would only reveal the senselessness of the general[22] and the folly of the writer who should select as praiseworthy the reckless imperilling of mighty interests. On the contrary, what I admire is the fact that he had taken care to provide himself with an army not inferior to that of his enemy, and had so equipped them that his cohorts literally gleamed with purple and bronze.[23] He had taken pains to enable his soldiers to undergo the fatigue of war, he had filled their breasts with a proud consciousness that they were equal to do battle with any combatants in the world, and what was more, he had infused a wholesome rivalry in those about him to prove themselves each better than the rest. He had filled all hearts with sanguine expectation of great blessings to descend on all, if they proved themselves good men. Such incentives, he thought, were best calculated to arouse enthusiasm in men's souls to engage in battle with the enemy. And in this expectation he was not deceived.

I proceed to describe the battle, for in certain distinctive features it differed from all the battles of our day. The contending forces met on the plain of Coronea, Agesilaus and his troops approaching from the Cephisus, the Thebans and their allies from the slopes of the Helicon. These masses of infantry, as any eye might see, were of duly balanced strength, while as near as could be the cavalry on either side was numerically the same. Agesilaus held the right of his own army, and on his extreme left lay the men of Orchomenus. On the opposite side the Thebans themselves formed their own right and the Argives held their left. While the two armies approached a deep silence prevailed on either side, but when they were now a single furlong's[24] space apart the Thebans quickened to a run, and, with a loud hurrah, dashed forward to close quarters. And now there was barely a hundred yards[25] between them, when Herippidas, with his foreign brigade, rushed forward from the Spartan's battle lines to meet them. This brigade consisted partly of troops which had served with Agesilaus ever since he left home, with a portion of the Cyreians, besides Ionians, Aeolians, and their neighbours on the Hellespont. All these took part in the forward rush of the attack just mentioned, and coming within spear-thrust they routed that portion of the enemy in front of them. The Argives did not even wait for Agesilaus and his division, but fled towards Helicon, and at that moment some of his foreign friends were on the point of crowning Agesilaus with the wreath of victory, when some one brought him word that the Thebans had cut through the division from Orchomenus and were busy with the baggage-train. Accordingly he at once deployed his division and advanced by counter-march against them. The Thebans on their side, seeing that their allies had scattered on Helicon, and eager to make their way back to join their friends, began advancing sturdily.

To assert that Agesilaus at this crisis displayed real valour is to assert a thing indisputable, but for all that the course he adopted was not the safest. It was open to him to let the enemy pass in their effort to rejoin their friends, and that done to have hung upon their heels and overmastered their rear ranks, but he did nothing of the sort: what he did was, to crash front to front against the Thebans. And so with shields interlocked they shoved and fought and fought and shoved, dealing death and yielding life. There was no shouting, nor yet was there even silence, but a strange and smothered utterance, such as rage and battle vent.[26] At last a portion of the Thebans forced their way through towards Helicon, but many were slain in that departure.

Victory remained with Agesilaus. Wounded himself, they bore him back to his own lines, when some of his troopers came galloping up to tell him that eighty of the enemy had taken refuge with their arms[27] under cover of the Temple,[28] and they asked what they ought to do. He, albeit he had received wounds all over him, having been the mark of divers weapons, did not even so forget his duty to God, and gave orders to let them go whithersoever they chose, nor suffered them to be ill-treated, but ordered his bodyguard of cavalry to escort them out of reach of danger.

And now that the battle had ceased, it was a sight to see where the encounter took place, the earth bedabbled with gore, the dead lying cheek by jowl, friend and foe together, and the great shields hacked and broken to pieces, and the spears snapped asunder, the daggers lying bare of sheaths, some on the ground, some buried in the bodies, some still clutched in the dead men's hands. For the moment then, seeing that it was already late in the day, they dragged together the corpses of their slain apart from those of the enemy[29] and laid them within the lines, and took their evening meal and slept; but early next morning Agesilaus ordered Gylis, the polemarch, to marshal the troops in battle order and to set up a trophy, while each man donned a wreath in honour of the god, and the pipers piped. So they busied themselves, but the Thebans sent a herald asking leave to bury their dead under cover of a truce. And so it came to pass that a truce was made, and Agesilaus departed homewards, having chosen, in lieu of supreme greatness in Asia, to rule, and to be ruled, in obedience to the laws at home.

It was after this[30] that his attention was drawn to the men of Argos. They had appropriated Corinth, and were reaping the fruits of their fields at home. The war to them was a merry jest. Accordingly he marched against them; and having ravaged their territory throughout, he crossed over by the pass[31] down upon Corinth and captured the long walls leading to Lechaeum. And so having thrown open the gates of Peloponnese he returned home in time for the Hyacinthia,[32] where, in the post assigned to him by the master of the chorus, he shared in the performance of the paean in honour of the god.

Later on, it being brought to his notice that the Corinthians were keeping all their cattle safely housed in the Peiraeum, sowing the whole of that district, and gathering in their crops; and, which was a matter of the greatest moment, that the

Boeotians, with Creusis as their base of operations, could pour their succours into Corinth by this route — he marched against Peiraeum. Finding it strongly guarded, he made as if the city of Corinth were about to capitulate, and immediately after the morning meal shifted his ground and encamped against the capital. Under cover of night there was a rush from Peiraeum to protect the city, which he was well aware of, and with break of day he turned right about and took Peiraeum, defenceless as it lay, capturing all that it contained, with the various fortresses within; and having so done retired homewards.

After these exploits[33] the Achaeans were urgent for an alliance, and begged him to join them in an expedition against Acarnania. In the course of this the Acarnanians attacked him in a defile. Storming the heights above his head with his light troops,[34] he gave them battle, and slew many of them, and set up a trophy, nor stayed his hand until he had united the Acarnanians, the Aetolians, and the Argives,[35] in friendship with the Achaeans and alliance with himself.

When the enemy, being desirous of peace, sent an embassy, it was Agesilaus who spoke against the peace,[36] until he had forced the states of Corinth and of Thebes to welcome back those of them who, for Lacedaemon's sake, had suffered banishment.

And still later,[37] again, he restored the exiles of the Phliasians, who had suffered in the same cause, and with that object marched in person against Phlius, a proceeding which, however liable to censure on other grounds, showed unmistakable attachment to his party.[38]

Thus, when the adverse faction had put to death those of the Lacedaemonians then in Thebes, he brought succour to his friends, and marched upon Thebes.[39] Finding the entire country fenced with ditch and palisading, he crossed Cynoscephalae[40] and ravaged the district right up to the city itself, giving the Thebans an opportunity of engaging him in the plain or upon the hills, as they preferred. And once more, in the ensuing year,[41] he marched against Thebes, and now surmounting these palisades and entrenchments at Scolus,[42] he ravaged the remainder of Boeotia.

Hitherto fortune had smiled in common upon the king himself and upon his city. And as for the disasters which presently befell, no one can maintain that they were brought about under the leadership of Agesilaus. But the day came when, after the disaster which had occurred at Leuctra, the rival powers in conjunction with the Mantineans fell to massacring his friends and adherents[43] in Tegea (the confederacy between all the states of Boeotia, the Arcadians, and the Eleians being already an accomplished fact). Thereupon, with the forces of Lacedaemon alone,[44] he took the field, and thus belied the current opinion that it would be a long while before the Lacedaemonians ventured to leave their own territory again. Having ravaged the country of those who had done his friends to death, he was content, and returned home.

After this Lacedaemon was invaded by the united Arcadians, Argives, Eleians, and Boeotians, who were assisted by the Phocians, both sections of the Locrians, the Thessalians, Aenianians, Acarnanians, and Euboeans; moreover, the slaves had revolted and several of the provincial cities;[45]while of the Spartans themselves as many had fallen on the field of Leuctra as survived. But in spite of all, he safely guarded the city, and that too a city without walls and bulwarks. Forbearing to engage in the open field, where the gain would lie wholly with the enemy, he lay stoutly embattled on ground where the citizens must reap advantage; since, as he doggedly persisted, to march out meant to be surrounded on every side; whereas to stand at bay where every defile gave a coign of vantage, would give him mastery complete.[46]

After the invading army had retired, no one will gainsay the sound sense of his behaviour. Old age debarred him from active service on foot or horse, and what the city chiefly needed now, he saw, was money, if she looked to gain allies. To the task therefore of providing that he set himself. Everything that could be done by stopping at home he deftly turned his hand to; or when the call arose and he could better help his country by departure he had no false pride; he set off on foreign service, not as general, but as ambassador. Yet on such embassy he achieved acts worthy of the greatest general. Autophradates[47] was besieging Ariobarzanes,[48] who was an ally of Sparta, in Assos; but before the face of Agesilaus he fled in terror and was gone. Cotys,[49] besieging Sestos, which still adhered to Ariobarzanes, broke up the siege and departed crestfallen. Well might the ambassador have set up a trophy in commemoration of the two bloodless victories. Once more, Mausolus[50] was besieging both the above-named places with a squadron of one hundred sail. He too, like, and yet unlike, the former two, yielded not to terror but to persuasion, and withdrew his fleet. These, then, were surely admirable achievements, since those who looked upon him as a benefactor and those who fled from before him both alike made him the richer by their gifts.

Tachos,[51] indeed, and Mausolus gave him a magnificent escort; and, for the sake of his former friendship with

Agesilaus, the latter contributed also money for the state of Lacedaemon; and so they sped him home.

And now the weight of, may be, fourscore years was laid upon him,[52] when it came under his observation that the king of Egypt,[53] with his hosts of foot and horse and stores of wealth, had set his heart on a war with Persia. Joyfully he learned that he himself was summoned by King Tachos, and that the command-inchief of all the forces was promised to him. By this one venture he would achieve three objects, which were to requite the Egyptian for the benefits conferred on Lacedaemon; to liberate the Hellenes in Asia once again; and to inflict on the Persian a just recompense, not only for the old offences, but for this which was of today; seeing that, while boasting alliance with Sparta, he had dictatorially enjoined the emancipation of Messene.[54] But when the man who had summoned him refused to confer the proffered generalship, Agesilaus, like one on whom a flagrant deception has been practised, began to consider the part he had to play. Meanwhile a separate division[55] of the Egyptian armies held aloof from their king. Then, the disaffection spreading, all the rest of his troops deserted him; whereat the monarch took flight and retired in exile to Sidon in Phoenicia, leaving the Egyptians, split in faction, to choose to themselves a pair of kings.[56] Thereupon Agesilaus took his decision. If he helped neither, it meant that neither would pay the service-money due to his Hellenes, that neither would provide a market, and that, whichever of the two conquered in the end, Sparta would be equally detested. But if he threw in his lot with one of them, that one would in all likelihood in return for the kindness prove a friend. Accordingly he chose between the two that one who seemed to be the truer partisan of Hellas, and with him marched against the enemy of Hellas and conquered him in a battle, crushing him. His rival he helped to establish on the throne, and having made him a friend to Lacedaemon, and having acquired vast sums besides, he turned and set sail homewards, even in mid-winter, hastening so that Sparta might not lie inactive, but against the coming summer be alert to confront the foe.

[18] I.e. "Xerxes."

[19] I.e. "the Three hundred." See Thuc. v. 72; "Pol. Lac." xiii. 6.

[20] See "Hell." IV. ii. 7.

[21] Lit. "mora."

[22] Lit. "Agesilaus."

23 See "Cyrop." VI. iv. 1.

24 Lit. "a stade."

25 Lit. "three plethra."

26 Or, "as the rage and fury of battle may give vent to." See "Cyrop." VII. i. 38-40. A graphic touch omitted in "Hell." IV. iii. 19.

27 I.e. "they had kept their arms."

28 See Plut. "Ages." xix.; Paus. ix. 34.

29 Reading, tous ek ton polemion nekrous, after Weiske.

30 B.C. 393.

31 kata ta stena. See "Hell." IV. iv. 19. kata Tenean, according to Koppen's emendation.

32 See Grote, "H. G." v. 208; Herod. ix. 7; "Hell." IV. v. 10.

33 B.C. 390-389?

34 See "Hell." IV. vi. 9-11, where it is expressly stated that the action was won by the Spartan hoplites. See Hartman, "An.

Xen." (cap. xi. "De Agesilao libello"), p. 263, for other discrepancies between the historian and the encomiast.

35 See perhaps "Hell." IV. iv. 19; vii. 2 foll.

36 I.e. "of Antalcidas, B.C. 387." See "Hell." V. i. 36; Grote, "H. G." ix. 537 note.

37 B.C. 383 and 380; see "Hell." V. ii. 10; iii. 10.

38 See "Hell." V. iii. 16.

39 B.C. 378.

40 See "Hell." V. iv. 34 foll.; for the site see Breitenbach, ad loc.

41 B.C. 377.

42 See "Hell." V. iv. 47.

43 Or intimates.

44 B.C. 370. See "Hell."VI. v. 21.

45 Lit. "perioecid"; see Plut. "Ages." xxxii. (Clough, iv. 39); "Hell." VI. v. 32.

46 Is this parallel to "Hell." VII. v. 10, or "Hell." VI. v. 28? According to the historian, Agesilaus adopted similar tactics

on both occasions (in B.C. 369 and B.C. 362 alike). The encomiast after his manner appears to treat them as one. Once and again his hero "cunctando restituit rem," but it was by the same strategy.

47 Satrap of Lydia.

48 Satrap of Propontis or Hellespontine Phrygia.

49 Satrap of Paphlagonia, king of Thrace. Iphicrates married his daughter. See Grote, "H. G." x. 410.

50 Satrap of Caria.

51 King of Egypt.

52 Or, "But to pass on, he was already, may be, eighty years of age, when it came under his observation . . . ."

53 This same Tachos.

54 See "Hell." VII. i. 36; iv. 9.

55 I.e. "the army under Nectanebos." See Diod. xv. 92; Plut. "Ages." xxxvii. (Clough, iv. 44 foll.)

56 I.e. "Nectanebos and a certain Mendesian."

III

Such, then, is the chronicle of this man's achievements, or of such of them as were wrought in the presence of a thousand witnesses. Being of this sort they have no need of further testimony; the mere recital of them is sufficient, and they at once win credence. But now I will endeavour to reveal the excellence indwelling in his soul, the motive power of his acts, in virtue of which he clung to all things honourable and thrust aside all baseness.

Agesilaus showed such reverence for things divine that even his enemies regarded his oaths and solemn treaties as more to be relied on than the tie of friendship amongst themselves. These same men, who would shrink from too close intercourse with one another, delivered themselves into the hands of Agesilaus without fear. And lest the assertion should excite discredit, I may name some illustrious examples. Such was Spithridates the Persian, who knew that Pharnabazus,[57] whilst negotiating to marry the daughter of the great king, was minded to seize his own daughter unwedded. Resenting such brutality, Spithridates delivered up himself, his wife, his children, and his whole power, into the hands of Agesilaus. Cotys[58] also, the ruler of Paphlagonia, had refused to obey a summons from the king, although he sent him the warrant of his right hand;[59] then fear came upon him lest he should be seized, and either be heavily fined or die the death; yet he too, simply trusting to an armistice, came to the camp of Agesilaus and made alliance, and of his own accord chose to take the field with Agesilaus, bringing a thousand horsemen and two thousand targeteers. Lastly, Pharnabazus[60] himself came and held colloquy with Agesilaus, and openly agreed that if he were not himself appointed general-inchief of the royal forces he would revolt from the king. "Whereas, if I do become general," he added, "I mean to make war upon you, Agesilaus, might and main," thus revealing his confidence that, say what he might, nothing would befall him contrary to the terms of truce. Of so intrinsic a value to all, and not least to a general in the field, is the proud possession of an honest and God-fearing character, known and recognised. Thus far, as touching the quality of piety.

[57] See "Hell." III. iv. 10; Plut. "Ages." xi. (Clough, iv. 9).

[58] See "Hell." IV. i. 3; Plut. "Ages." xi. (Clough, iv. 13).

[59] Diod. xvi. 34.

[60] See "Hell." IV. i. 37.

IV

To speak next of his justice[61] in affairs of money. As to this, what testimony can be more conclusive than the following? During the whole of his career no charge of fraudulent dealing was ever lodged against Agesilaus; against which set the many-voiced acknowledgment of countless benefits received from him. A man who found pleasure in giving away his own for the benefit of others was not the man to rob another of his goods at the price of infamy. Had he suffered from this thirst for riches it would have been easier to cling to what belonged to him than to take that to which he had no just title. This man, who was so careful to repay debts of gratitude, where[62] the law knows no remedy against defaulters, was not likely to commit acts of robbery which the law regards as criminal. And as a matter of act Agesilaus judged it not only wrong to forgo repayment of a deed of kindness, but, where the means were ample, wrong also not to repay such debts with ample interest.

The charge of embezzlement, could it be alleged, would no less outrage all reason in the case of one who made over to his country the benefit in full of grateful offerings owed solely to himself. Indeed the very fact that, when he wished to help the city or his friends with money, he might have done so by the aid of others, goes a long way to prove his indifference to the lure of riches; since, had he been in the habit of selling his favour, or of playing the part of benefactor for pay, there had been no room for a sense of indebtedness.[63] It is only the recipient of gratuitous kindness who is ever ready to minister to his benefactor, both in return for the kindness itself and for the confidence implied in his selection as the fitting guardian of a good deed on deposit.[64]

Again, who more likely to put a gulf impassable between himself and the sordid love of gain[65] than he, who nobly preferred to be stinted of his dues[66] rather than snatch at the lion's share unjustly? It is a case in point that, being pronounced by the state to be the rightful heir to his brother's[67] wealth, he made over one half to his maternal relatives because he saw that they were in need; and to the truth of this assertion all Lacedaemon is witness. What, too, was his answer to Tithraustes when the satrap offered him countless gifts if he would but quit the country? "Tithraustes, with us it is deemed nobler for a ruler to enrich his army than himself; it is expected of him to wrest spoils from the enemy rather than take gifts."

[61] See Muller and Donaldson, "Hist. Gk. Lit." ii. 196, note 2.

62 Or, "a state of indebtedness beyond the reach of a tribunal." See "Cyrop." I. ii. 7.

63 Or, "no one would have felt to owe him anything."

64 See "Cyrop." VI. i. 35; Rutherford, "New Phrynichus," p. 312.

65 Or, "base covetousness."

66 Or reading, sun auto to gennaio (with Breitenbach), "in obedience to pure generosity." See "Cyrop." VIII. iii. 38.

67 I.e. Agis. See Plut. "Ages." iv.

V

Or again, reviewing the divers pleasures which master human beings, I defy any one to name a single one to which Agesilaus was enslaved: Agesilaus, who regarded drunkenness as a thing to hold aloof from like madness, and immoderate eating like the snare of indolence. Even the double portion[68] allotted to him at the banquet was not spent on his own appetite; rather would be make distribution of the whole, retaining neither portion for himself. In his view of the matter this doubling of the king's share was not for the sake of surfeiting, but that the king might have the wherewithal to honour whom he wished. And so, too, sleep[69] he treated not as a master, but as a slave, subservient to higher concerns. The very couch he lay upon must be sorrier than that of any of his company or he would have blushed for shame, since in his opinion it was the duty of a leader to excel all ordinary mortals in hardihood, not in effeminacy. Yet there were things in which he was not ashamed to take the lion's share, as, for example, the sun's heat in summer, or winter's cold. Did occasion ever demand of his army moil and toil, he laboured beyond all others as a thing of course, believing that such ensamples are a consolation to the rank and file. Or, to put the matter compendiously, Agesilaus exulted in hard work: indolence he utterly repudiated.

And, as touching the things of Aphrodite, if for nothing else, at any rate for the marvel of it, the self-restraint of the man deserves to be put on record. It is easy to say that to abstain from that which excites no desire is but human; yet in the case of Megabates, the son of Spithridates, he was moved by as genuine a love as any passionate soul may feel for what is lovely. Now, it being a national custom among the Persians to salute those whom they honour with a kiss, Megabates endeavoured so to salute Agesilaus, but the latter with much show of battle, resisted —"No kiss might he accept."[70] I ask whether such an incident does not reveal on the face of it the self-respect of the man, and that of no vulgar order.[71]Megabates, who looked upon himself as in some sense dishonoured, for the future endeavoured not to offend in like sort again.[72] Whereupon Agesilaus appealed to one who was his comrade to persuade Megabates again to honour him with his regard; and the comrade, so appealed to, demanding, "If I persuade him, will you bestow on him a kiss?" Agesilaus fell into a silence, but presently exclaimed: "No, by the Twins, not if I might this very instant become the swiftest-footed, strongest, and handsomest of men.[73] And as to that battle I swear by all the gods I would far rather fight it over again than that everything on which I set my eyes might turn to gold."[74]

What construction some will put upon the story I am well aware, but for myself I am persuaded that many more people can master their enemeis than the foes we speak of.[75] Doubtless such incidents when known to but few may well be discredited by many, but here we are in the region of establishing facts, seeing that the more illustrious a man is the less can his every act escape notice. As to Agesilaus no eye-witness has ever reported any unworthy behaviour, nor, had he invented it, would his tale have found credence, since it was not the habit of the king, when abroad, to lodge apart in private houses. He always lay up in some sacred place, where behaviour of the sort was out of the question, or else in public, with the eyes of all men liable to be called as witnesses to his sobriety. For myself, if I make these statements falsely against the knowledge of Hellas, this were not in any sense to praise my hero, but to dispraise myself.

[68] See "Pol. Lac." xv. 4. See J. J. Hartman, "An. Xen." 257.

[69] See Hom. "Il." ii. 24, ou khro pannukhion eudein boulephoron andra, "to sleep all night through beseemeth not one that is a counsellor."— W. Leaf.

[20] See Plut. "Ages." (Clough, iv. p. 13 foll.)

[21] Reading, kai lian gennikon; or, "a refinement of self-respect," "a self-respect perhaps even over-sensitive."

[22] Lit. "made no further attempt to offer kisses."

[23] See Plut. "Ages." ii. (Clough, iv. p. 2): "He is said to have been a little man of a contemptible presence."

[24] See Plut. "Ages." xi. (Clough, iv. p. 14); "Parall. Min." v; Ovid. "Met." xi. 102 foll.

[25] Or, "than the seductions in question."

VI

Nor, in my opinion, were those obscure proofs of courage and true manliness which he furnished by his readiness ever to wage war against the strongest enemies, whether of Sparta or of Hellas, placing himself in the forefront of the contests decided on. If the enemy cared to join issue in fair field he would not chance upon a victory won by panic, but in stubborn battle, blow for blow, he mastered him; and set up trophies worthy of the name, seeing that he left behind him imperishable monuments of prowess, and bore away on his own body indelible marks of the fury with which he fought;[76] so that, apart from hearsay, by the evidence of men's eyes his valour stood approved.

And amongst these we must not deem them trophies alone which he actually set up, but reckon the many campaigns which he undertook, since they were victories truly, even when the enemy refused to encounter him, victories devoid of danger, yet fraught with even more solid advantage to the state of Sparta and her fellow-combatants; just as in our games we crown as victor him who walks over the field[zz] no less than him who conquers by dint of battle.

And to speak next of his wisdom,[78] I suppose there is not one of all his doings but must illustrate it; — this man whose bearing towards his fatherland was such that by dint of implicit obedience [he grew to so greate a height of power],[79] whose zeal in the service of his comrades won for him the unhesitating attachment of his friends, who infused into the hearts of his soldiers a spirit, not of discipline only, but of self-devotion to their chief. And yet surely that is the strongest of all battle-lines[80] in which obedience creates tactical efficieny, and alacrity in the field springs out of loyal affection for the general.

Enemies he had to cope with, who had little excuse to disparage, however much they might be compelled to hate their opponent, seeing that he was for ever contriving to give his allies some advantage over them — by sheer deception, if occasion offered; now anticipating them if speed were requisite; now skulking in corners if concealment served; in all points observing one rule of behaviour to his friends and another towards his foes. By turning night into day and day into night[81] he drew so close a veil of mystery over his movements that frequently there was no saying where he was, or whither he would go, or what he might do next. The fastnesses of the enemy he transformed into so many weaknesses,[82] passing this one by, and scaling that, and stealing like a thief into a third.

When he was on the march, and was well aware that an enemy might, if he chose, deliver battle, his habit was to lead his troops in compact battle order ready to confront emergencies, with soft, slow step, advancing, as it were, with maidenly demureness,[83] for in such procedure, as he believed, lay the secret of true calm, engendering a dauntless self-assurance, imperturbable, unerring, impervious to treacherous assault. Therefore by such behaviour he was a terror to the enemy, whilst he infused courage and strength in the hearts of his friends, so that throughout his life he continued to be a man whom his foes dared not despise, whom his fellow-citizens cared not to arraign, within the circle of his friends held blameless, the idol and admiration of the outer world.[84]

[76] Or, "visible signs of the spirit," etc. See Plut. "Ages." xxxvi.

[77] Or, "without striking a blow." Lit. "without the dust of the arena, 'sine pulvere.'" See Thuc. iv. 73, akoniti.

[78] Or, "his sagacity."

79 The words pleiston iskhue are supplied from Plutarch ("Ages." iv.), who quotes the passage, "What Xenophon tells us of him, that by complying with, and, as it were, ruled by his country, he grew into such great power with them, that he could do what he pleased, is meant," etc. (Clough, iv. p. 4). The lacuna in the MS. was first noted, I believe, by Weiske. See Breitenbach's note ad loc.

80 See "Cyrop." VII. i. 30; "Econ." xxi. 7.

81 See "Hell." VI. i. 15; "Pol. Lac." v. 7; "Cyrop." I. v. 12.

82 Or, "the strongholds of the enemy might to all intents and purposes have been open places."

83 See above, ii. 3; "Pol. Lac." iii. 5.

84 Cf. Tacitus's phrase concerning Titus, "deliciae humani generis."

VII

To describe his patriotism[85] point by point in detail were a tedious story, since, as I suppose, there is not one of his several achievements but must finally resolve itself into that. For, to put it briefly, we all know well that where Agesilaus expected in any way to benefit his country there was no toil he shrank from, no danger he avoided, no money he stinted, no excuse whether of age or body he admitted, but deemed it ever the true function of a good king[86] to shower blessings to the utmost on the subjects of his rule.

And for my part I hold it as chief among the magnificent benefits so conferred by him upon his country that, being the most powerful member of the state, he made no secret of his absolute submission to the laws,[87]since what lesser man, seeing the king's obedience, would take[88] on himself to disobey? Who, in discontentment at his own poor lot, would venture on revolution, knowing that the king himself could condescend to constitutional control? And that, too, a king who bore himself towards political opponents with a paternal mildness.[89] If he rebuked them sharply for their misdemeanours, he none the less honoured their high endeavours, and proved himself a present help to them in time of trouble.[90] No citizen could be his personal foe; of that he was assured. His desire was to commend them one and all alike, counting the common salvation of all a gain, and reckoning it as a loss if even a mean man perished. For thus he reasoned, nor made a secret of the conclusion he had come to: so long as her citizens continued tranquilly adherent to the laws the happiness of Sparta was secure.[91] And for the rest Sparta would once again be strong on that day when the states of Hellas should learn wisdom.

And if, by admission, it is noble for every Hellene to be a lover of his fellow-Hellenes, yet we must fare far afield to find another instance of a general who, expecting to sack some city, would have refused to seize the prize; or who regarded victory in a war waged against fellow-Hellenes as a species of calamity. Yet this man when a message was brought him concerning the battle at Corinth,[92] in which but eight Lacedaemonians had fallen, but of their opponents ten thousand nearly, showed no sign of exultation, but sighed, saying, "Alas for Hellas! since those who now lie in their graves, were able, had they lived, to conquer the hosts of Asia."[93] Again, when some Corinthian exiles informed him that their city was ripe for surrender, and showed him the engines by which they were confident they would take the walls, he refused to make the assault, saying that Hellene cities ought not to be reduced to slavery, but brought back to a better mind,[94] and added, "For if we lop off our offending members, haply we may deprive ourselves of the means to master the barbarians."

Again, if it is a sacred duty to hate the Persian, who of old set out on a campaign to enslave Hellas; the Persian, who today makes alliance with these (no matter to him which the party, provided it will help him to work the greater mischief[95]); or gives presents to those (who will take them and do the greatest harm to his foes the Hellenes); or else concocts a peace that shall presently involve us in internecine war, as he anticipates:— but why dwell on facts so patent? — I ask, did ever Hellene before Agesilaus so enter heart and soul upon his duty; whether it were to help some tribe to throw off the Persian yoke, or to save from destruction a revolted district, or if nothing else, at any rate to saddle the Persian with such troubles of his own that he should cease to trouble Hellas? An ardent hater of Persia surely was he, who, when his own country was at war with Hellenes, did not neglect the common good of Hellas, but set sail to wreak what harm he might upon the barbarians.[96]

[85] Lit. "love for his own city."

86 Or, "regarded it as the cardinal virtue of a real prince." See "Mem." III. ii. 3.

87 Or, "he was at the same time the most obvious in his allegiance to the laws."

88 Lit. "would have taken on himself . . . would have ventured on revolution."

89 Lit. "as a father to his children."

90 Or, "and was ready to stand by their side in time of trouble."

91 Or, "For this was the clear tenor of his thought, that by tranquil continuance within the laws the citizens of Sparta might secure her happiness. And as to power, Sparta, etc." See "Mem." II. vi. 27.

92 B.C. 394. See "Hell." IV. ii. 9-23; Diod. xiv. 83; Grote, "H. G." ix. 429.

93 Lit. "all the barbarians."

94 See "Econ." i. 23.

95 Or, "the worse the mischief he can work, the better the side."

96 See Isocr. "Ep." ix. "To Archidamus," S. 11-14.

VIII

To turn to another side, that grace of manner which was his, claims more than passing recognition. Here was a man to whom honour was vouchsafed and power present, and who, to crown all else, held in his hands the sceptre of sovereignty — a kingship not plotted against, but respected and beloved. Yet there was no trace of arrogance to be seen in him, but of tender affection and courteous service to his friends proof in abundance without seeking. Witness the zest with which he shared in the round of lovers' talk;[97] the zeal with which he threw himself into the serious concerns[98] of friends. By dint of a hopeful and cheery disposition and unflagging gaiety of heart he attracted to his side a throng of visitors, who came, not simply for the transaction of some private interest, but rather to pass away the day in pleasant sort. Though little apt himself to use high-swelling words, it did not annoy him to hear others sounding their own praises, which he regarded as a harmless weakness, the pledge at least of high endeavour[99] in the future.

But that he was capable of lofty sentiment and at the right season must not be overlooked. Thus when a letter reached him from the king (I speak of that which was brought by the

Persian agent in company with Calleas[100] of Lacedaemon, proposing terms of hospitality and friendship with the Persian monarch), he disdained to accept it, telling the bearer to take back to the king this answer: "He need not be at pains to send him letters in private, but if he could prove himself a friend to Lacedaemon and the well-wisher of Hellas he should have no cause to blame the ardour of his friendship," but added, "if your king be detected plotting, let him not think to find a friend in me. No, not if he sends me a thousand letters." For my part, then, I hold it praiseworthy that, by comparison with pleasing his fellow-Hellenes, Agesilaus scorned such friendship. And this, too, among his tenets I find admirable: the truer title to self-congratulation belonged not to the millionaire, the master of many legions, but to him rather, who, being himself a better man, commanded the allegience of better followers.

And this, in proof of mental forecast, I must needs praise in him. Holding to the belief that the more satraps there were who revolted from the king the surer the gain to Hellas, he did not suffer himself to be seduced, either by gifts or by the mightiness in his power, to be drawn into bonds of friendship with the king, but took precaution rather not to abuse their confidence who were willing to revolt.

And lastly, as beyond all controversy admirable, note this contrast: First, the Persian, who, believing that in the multitude of his riches he had power to lay all things under his feet, would fain have swept into his coffers all the gold and all the silver of mankind: for him, and him alone, the costliest and most precious things of earth. And then this other, who contrariwise so furnished his establishment as to be totally independent of every adventitious aid.[101] And if any one doubts the statement, let him look and see with what manner of dwelling-place he was contented; let him view the palace doors: these are the selfsame doors, he might well imagine, which Aristodemus,[102] the great-great-grandson of Heracles, took and set up in the days of the return. Let him endeavour to view the furniture inside; there he will perceive how the king feasted on high holy days; and he will hear how the king's own daughter was wont to drive to Amyclae in a public basket-carriage.[103] Thus it was that by the adjustment of expenditure to income he was never driven to the commission of any unjust deed for money's sake. And yet if it be a fine thing to hold a fortress impregnable to attack, I count it a greater glory that a man should hold the fortress of his soul inviolable against the assaults of riches, pleasures, fears.

97 See "Hell." V. iii. 20; "Cyrop." I. iv. 27; "Econ." ii. 7; Plut. "Ages." ii.; xx.; Lyc. xx.

98 Or, "he would discuss graver matters, according to the humour of his friends."

99 Or, "of courageous conduct," "noble manhood."

100 See "Hell." IV. i. 15; Plut. "Apophth. Lac." p. 777; Grote, "H. G." x. 402.

101 Or, "of all such external needs."

102 See Herod. vi. 52.

103 See Plut. "Ages." xix. (Clough, iv. p. 23); the words e thugater autouwere supplied from this passage by Casaubon.

IX

I will here state to what extent the style of living which he presented stands out in striking contrast to the ostentatious manner of the Persian.[104] In the first place, if the latter made a solemn affectation of being but seldom seen, Agesilaus delighted to live in the eye of day, believing that seclusion might accord well enough as a screen for shameless conduct, but to a life of nobleness and beauty[105] heaven's light added new ornament.[106] And next, if the one prided himself on being unapproachable, the other rejoiced in being accessible to all the world; the one, with his airs and graces, was pleased to transact business slowly, the other was never so happy as when he could satisfy the demands of a petitioner without waste of time.[107]

Again, it is worthy of observation how much easier and simpler to satisfy was the standard of comfort which the Spartan aimed at.[108] For the Persian, men must compass sea and land to discover some beverage which he will care to drink; he needs ten thousand pastrycooks to supply the kick-shaws he will deign to eat; and to procure him the blessing of sleep no tongue can describe what a world of trouble must be taken.

But Agesilaus was a lover of toil, and therefore not so dainty; the meanest beverage was sweet to his lips, and pleasant enough to his taste was the chance fare of the moment; and for the purpose of refreshing slumber every place alike conducive. It was not merely that to fare thus gave him pure pleasure, but in the sense of contrast lay a double satisfaction. Here was he roaming earth freely in the midst of a world of delight,[109] and there lay the Persian, under his eyes, who to escape a life of pain must drag together from the uttermost parts of earth the separate ingredients for his pleasure. It was another source of joy that to himself it was given to confront the appointed order of the universe[110] without pain; while through weakness of soul his rival, it was plain to see, was driven to flee away from heat and cold, and to shape his life, not by the pattern of brave men, but of some mean and defenceless animal.[111]

And what a fine trait this was in him, and betokening how lofty a sentiment, that, being content to adorn his own house with works and possessions suited to a man, and being devoted to the breeding of dogs and horses in large numbers for the chase and warfare, he persuaded his sister Cynisca to rear chariot horses,[112] and thus by her victory[113] showed that to keep a stud of that sort, however much it might be a mark of wealth, was hardly a proof of manly virtue. And surely in the following opinion we may discern plainly the generosity of him who entertained it. To win victories over private persons in a chariot race does not add one tittle to a man's renown. He, rather, who holds his city dear beyond all things else, who has himself sunk deep into the heart of her affections, who has obtained to himself all over the world a host of friends and those the noblest, who can outdo his country and comrades alike in the race of kindliness, and his antagonists in vengeance — such a man may, in a true sense, be said to bear away the palm of victory in conquests noble and magnificent; living and in death to him belongs transcendent fame.

[104] Or, "how he presented his own manner in antithesis to the false pretences of the Persian." For alazoneia see "Mem." I. vii. 1; Aristot. "N. E." iv. 7; Theophr. "Char." vi.

[105] Lit. "a life striving towards beauteousness."

[106] Or, "added but greater lustre."

[107] Lit. "could satisfy and dismiss his petitioners without delay."

[108] See Herod. i. 135, for the luxury of the Persians and for the refinements of civilisation. See "Mem." II. i. 10; "Cyrop." VIII. i. 40.

¹⁰⁹ Or, "in a round of festivity."

¹¹⁰ See Plut. "Ages." xiv. (Clough, iv. p. 17); "Apophth. Lac." p. 102; Eur. "Supp." 214, 215.

de ou truphomen, theou kataskeuen bio dontos toiauten, oisin ouk arkei tade;

¹¹¹ Or, "the most defenceless of God's creatures." Lit. "the weakest of animals."

¹¹² I.e. "for the games."

¹¹³ I.e. "at Olympia." Cynisca, according to Pausanias (iii. 8), was the first woman who won a prize at Olympia. See also Plut. "Ages." xx. (Clough, iv. p. 23).

X

It is as possessing qualities such as these that I praise Agesilaus. And in these matters he was not like a man who chances upon a treasure and thereby becomes wealthier, albeit none the more skilful in economy; nor yet like him who, when a plague has fallen upon an enemy, wrests a victory, whereby he may add to his reputation for success, but not for strategy. Rather was his example that of one who in each emergency will take the lead; at a crisis where toil is needful, by endurance; or in the battle-lists of bravery by prowess; or when the function of the counsellor is uppermost, by the soundness of his judgment. Of such a man I say, he has obtained by warrant indefeasible the title peerless.

And if, as a means towards good workmanship, we count among the noble inventions of mankind the rule and the plummet,[114] no less happily shall we, who desire to attain a manly excellence, find in the virtue of Agesilaus a pattern and example. He was God-fearing, he was just in all his dealings, sound of soul and self-controlled. How then shall we who imitate him become his opposite, unholy, unjust, tyrannical, licentious? And, truth to say, this man prided himself, not so much on being a king over others as on ruling himself,[115] not so much on leading his citizens to attack the enemy as on guiding them to embrace all virtue.

Yet let it not be supposed, because he whom we praise has finished life, that our discourse must therefore be regarded as a funeral hymn.[116]Far rather let it be named a hymn of praise, since in the first place it is only the repetition, now that he is dead, of a tale familiar to his ears when living. And in the next place, what is more remote from dirge and lamentation than a life of glory crowned by seasonable death? What more deserving of song and eulogy than resplendent victories and deeds of highest note? Surely if one man rather than another may be accounted truly blest, it is he who, from his boyhood upwards, thirsted for glory, and beyond all contemporary names won what he desired; who, being gifted with a nature most emulous of honour, remained from the moment he was king unconquered; who attained the fullest term of mortal life and died without offence[117] committed, whether as concerning those at whose head he marched, or as towards those others against whom he fought in war.

[114] See Aeschin. "c. Ctes." p. 52, 25; Plat. "Phileb." 56 B.

[115] See Plut. "Apophth. Lac." p. 104.

116 See Symonds' "Greek Poets," ch. v.

117 As to the word anamartetos so translated, see Breitenbach, Exc. ad x. 4 of his edition.

XI

It only remains for me, under the form of headings,[118] to review the topic of this great man's virtue, in hopes that thus his eulogy may cling to the memory more lastingly.

Agesilaus reverenced the shrines and sacred places even of the enemy. We ought, he said, to make the gods our allies on hostile no less than on friendly soil.

He would do no violence to a suppliant, no, not even if he were his own foe; since how irrational must it be to stigmatise robbers of temples as sacrilegious and yet to regard him who tears the suppliant from the altar as a pious person.

One tenet he never wearied of repeating: the gods, he said, are not less pleased with holy deeds than with pure victims.

In the day of his prosperity his thoughts were not raised higher than befits a man; he gave thanks to the gods; and offered more victims when he had nothing to fear than he registered vows in time of apprehension.

He was accustomed in the midst of anxiety to wear an aspect of gaiety, but, when the victory was won, of gentleness.

Amongst friends his warmest greeting was reserved, not for the most powerful, but for the most ardent; and if he hated, it was not him who, being evil entreated, retaliated, but one who, having had kindness done to him, seemed incapable of gratitude.

He rejoiced when sordid greed was rewarded with poverty; and still more if he might himself enrich a righteous man, since his wish was to render uprightness more profitable than iniquity.

He made it a practice to associate with all kinds of people, but to be intimate only with the best.

As he listened to the praise of this man, or the censure of another, he felt that he learnt quite as much about the character of the speakers themselves as of those whom they discussed.

To be cheated by a friend was scarcely censurable, but he could find no condemnation strong enough for him who was outwitted by a foe. Or again, to dupe the incredulous might argue wit, but to take in the unsuspecting was veritably a crime.

The praise of a critic who had courage to point out his defects pleased him; and plainness of speech excited in him no hostility. It was against the cunning rather of the secretive person that he guarded himself, as against a hidden snare.

The calumniator he detested more than the robber or the thief, in proportion as the loss of friends is greater than the loss of money.[119]

"Who steals my purse steals trash; 'tis something, nothing; 'Twas mine, 'tis his, and has been slave to thousands; But he that filches from me my good name Robs me of that which not enriches him And makes me poor indeed."

The errors of private persons he bore with gently, but those of rulers he looked upon as grave; since the mischief wrought in the one case was so small, and so large in the other. The proper attribute of royalty was, he maintained, not an avoidance of responsibility, but a constant striving after nobleness.[120]

Whilst he would not suffer any image[121] of his bodily form to be set up (though many wished to present him with a statue), he never ceased elaborating what should prove the monument of his spirit, holding that the former is the business of a statuary, the latter of one's self. Wealth might procure the one, he said, but only a good man could produce the other.

As for riches, he employed them not with justice merely, but with liberality, holding that for a just man it is sufficient if he let alone the things of others, but of a liberal man it is required that he should take of his own and give to supply another's needs.

He was ever subject to religious fear,[122] believing that no man during his lifetime, however well he lives, can be counted happy; it is only he who has ended his days with glory of whom it can be said that he has attained at last to blessedness.[123]

In his judgment it was a greater misfortune to neglect things good and virtuous, knowing them to be so, than in ignorance. Nor was he enamoured of any reputation, the essentials of which he had not laboriously achieved.[124]

He was one of the small band, as it seemed to me, who regard virtue, not as a thing to be patiently endured,[125] but as a supreme enjoyment. At any rate, to win the praise of mankind gave him a deeper pleasure than the acquisition of wealth; and he preferred to display courage far rather in conjunction with prudence than with unnecessary risks, and to cultivate wisdom in action more than by verbal discussion.

Very gentle to his friends, to his enemies he was most terrible. Whilst he could hold out against toil and trouble with the best, nothing pleased him better than yielding to his comrades. But passion was kindled in him by beauty of deed rather than of person.[126]

Skilled in the exercise of self-command in the midst of external welfare, he could be stout of heart enough in stress of danger.

Urbanity he practised, not with jest and witticisim, but by the courtesy of his demeanour.

In spite of a certain haughtiness, he was never overbearing, but rich in saving common sense. At any rate, while pouring contempt upon arrogance, he bore himself more humbly than the most ordinary man. In fact, what he truly took a pride in was the simplicity of his own attire, in contrast with the splendid adornment of his troops; or, again, in the paucity of his own wants, combined with a bountiful liberality towards his friends.

Besides all this, as an antagonist he could hit hard enough, but no one ever bore a lighter hand when the victory was won.[127]

The same man, whom an enemy would have found it hard to deceive, was pliability itself in the concerns of his friends. Whilst for ever occupied in laying these on a secure foundation, he made it a ceaseless task to baffle the projects of the national foe.

The epithets applied to him are significant. His relatives found in him a kinsman who was more than kind. To his intimates he appeared as a friend in need who is a friend indeed. To the man who had done him some service, of tenacious memory. To the victim of injustice, a knight-errant. And to those who had incurred danger by his side, a saviour second only to the gods.

It was given to this man, as it appears to me, to prove exceptionally that though strength of body may wax old the vigour of a man's soul is exempt from eld. Of him, at any rate, it is true that he never shrank from the pursuit of great and noble objects, so long as[128] his body was able to support the vigour of his soul. Therefore his old age appeared mightier than the youth of other people. It would be hard to discover, I imagine, any one who in the prime of manhood was as formidable to his foes as Agesilaus when he had reached the limit of mortal life. Never, I suppose, was there a foeman whose removal came with a greater sense of relief to the enemy than that of Agesilaus, though a veteran when he died. Never was there a leader who inspired stouter courage in the hearts of fellow-combatants than this man with one foot planted in the grave. Never was a young man snatched from a circle of loving friends with tenderer regret than this old graybeard.

The benefactor of his fatherland, absolutely to the very end; with bounteous hand, even in the arms of death, dealing out largesse[129] to the city which he loved. And so they bore him home to his eternal resting-place;[130] this hero, who, having raised to himself many a monument of his valour over the broad earth, came back to find in the land of his fathers a sepulture worthy of a king.[131]

[118] Or, as others think, "in a summary."

[119] Mr. R. W. Taylor aptly quotes "Othello," III. iii. 157 —

[120] On the word kalokagathia so translated, see Demosth. 777, 5.

[121] See Plut. "Ages." ii. (Clough, iv. p. 2); also Plut. "Ap. Lac." p. 115; ib. p. 103; Cic. "ad Div." V. xii. 7.

[122] See "Cyr." III. iii. 58, and for the word deisidaimon, see Jebb, "Theophr. Char." p. 263 foll.; Mr. Ruskin, Preface to "Bibl. Past." vol. i. p. xxv.

[123] See Herod. i. 34; Soph. "Oed. Tyr." 1529; and Prof. Jebb's note ad loc.

[124] Or, "for which he did not qualify himself by the appropriate labour."

125 Or, "as a system of stoical endurance," "a kind of stoicism." But we must not let Xenophon, who is a Socratic, talk of the Stoa. If we knew certainly that the chapter was a much later production, the language would be appropriate enough.

126 Or, "beauteous deeds rather than bodily splendour."

127 Lit. "he was the heaviest of antagonists and the lightest of conquerors."

128 Reading, megalon kai kalon ephiemenos, eos kai to soma, k.t.l. See Breitenbach.

129 See above, ii. 31.

130 See for this remarkable phrase, Diod. i. 51.

131 See "Pol. Lac." xv. 9.

Notes

Notes

Printed in Great Britain
by Amazon